Don't Give Up

A 7-DAY DEVOTIONAL
JOURNEY FOR WOMEN

Don't Give Up

A 7-DAY DEVOTIONAL JOURNEY FOR WOMEN

ERICA N. WILLIAMS

Scripture quotations are taken from the *Holy Bible*, New Living Translation, copyright ©1996, 2004, 2015 by Tyndale House Foundation. Used by permission of Tyndale House Publishers, Inc., Carol Stream, Illinois 60188. All rights reserved.

Published by Erica N. Williams, LLC, Woodbridge, VA
Editorial Direction and Editing: Michele P. Roseman
Cover and Book Design: Josep Book Designs (joseworkwork@gmail.com)
Author Photo: MiniCrop, LLC

Printed in the United States of America
ISBN: 978-0-578-52230-2 (Print)

CONTENTS

To anyone who has ever felt like they weren't good enough and wanted to give up, I understand. That's why it's so important for us to know how God sees us and to rest in His unconditional love, security and hope. My sincere prayer is that as you work through the pages of this devotional, you'll comprehend even more deeply that you are loved unconditionally by God; He deems you worthy and valuable and has a great plan for your life.

As long as you follow Christ, you have no need to fear.

Day 1

PURE UNDERSTANDING OF GOD'S LEADERSHIP

Read: Matthew 16:24

"Then Jesus said to His disciples, "If any of you wants to be my follower, you must give up your own way, take up your cross, and follow me."" - Matthew 16:24 NLT

The year 2017 was the time when life threw more than a few curve balls my way. Seemingly, whenever I received good news -- and had just cause to celebrate -- shortly thereafter, I received bad news that left me at a loss for words. I'm sure you've been there before, right? One day you're sitting on top of the world, and the next day you're hit with a major problem that you can't solve.

This journey called life is filled with many turns and unexpected moments. Things don't always work out as planned. You must be patient, humble and focus as you take up your cross and follow Christ. No matter how difficult life's journey is, you must continue to remain hopeful and believe that God is working everything out for your good.

The Bible is filled with perfect examples of women who overcame the odds and pushed past their comfort levels to do what they were called to do. Many of them made incredible sacrifices. Esther, Abigail, Huldah, Lydia, Puah and Shiphrah are reminders that the odds will not always be in your favor, but you can overcome them. Success in life comes to those who face their difficult circumstances head-on and refuse to give up. It will require you to decide that you want God's will for your life—no matter what. Yes, the unknown is scary, but know that God understands your fears, weaknesses, insecurities, disappointments and your temptations. He may give you more than you can bear by yourself, but He'll always be there to help you come through (1 Corinthians 10:13).

PRAYER

Father, You are my strength and shield. You have not given me a spirit of fear, but of power, love, and a sound mind. Because of Your Son Jesus, there is not a challenge that I cannot overcome. I choose to take up my cross and follow You. Amen.

REFLECTION

Do you know that, as a Believer, God has given you the Holy Spirit to lead and guide you on your life journey? Are you sensitive to His Spirit? How can you commit to listening to the Spirit's direction today?

God is
working
things out
for you even
when you
don't feel it.

Day 2

PURE UNDERSTANDING OF GOD'S FAITHFULNESS

Read: Exodus 6

"I will claim you as my own people, and I will be your God. Then you will know that I am the Lord your God who has freed you from your oppression in Egypt." - Exodus 6:7 NLT

Have you ever received a promise from God that took forever to come to fruition? Sometimes you feel as though what God has promised isn't coming— due to the waiting process or the pain you've endured while waiting. The Israelites are an example of this dilemma. They didn't believe Moses due to the harshness of the slavery they endured while waiting to be delivered from the Egyptians.

Just imagine being told that you would be set free from slavery and given your own land. However, the person sent to speak on your behalf makes the situation worse by upsetting your master. He then increases your workload. The Israelites probably told Moses, "Man, God been promised us that we'd receive land because of His covenant with Abraham, Isaac, and Jacob oh so long ago, but we still haven't received it. Plus, we're being punished even more! We don't need you."

Just like the Israelites, there are likely times when your hurts and fears can close your ears to the hopeful words of God. Nonetheless, the Lord doesn't stop speaking to you when it's hard for you to hear. He continues working on your behalf just as He did in delivering His people from Egypt. God is all-powerful and will fulfill His promises. Keep these words in your heart and trust that God will do what He said He will do.

PRAYER

Father, I know it is difficult to wait. Strengthen me with Your Spirit and keep me focused on You as I patiently wait for You to fulfill Your promises in Your time. Amen.

REFLECTION

Are you waiting for God to fulfill a promise? How does today's passage impact you as you are waiting?

_____

_____

_____

_____

_____

_____

_____

_____

_____

_____

_____

_____

_____

_____

_____

_____

_____

_____

_____

_____

_____

_____

_____

Life isn't about finding yourself but discovering who God created you to be.

Day 3

PURE UNDERSTANDING
OF GOD'S PURPOSE

Read: Romans 8:29 – 39

*"And having chosen them, he called them to come to Him.
And having called them, He gave them right standing with
Himself. And having given them right standing, He gave them
His glory. What shall we say about such wonderful things as
these? If God is for us, who can ever be against us?" - Romans
8:30-31 NLT*

God has gifted Believers with spiritual gifts, talents and abilities that
will bring Him Glory; however, it's up to us to surrender and fulfill
His desires for our lives. To do this, we must begin to see ourselves as
Christ sees us.

1 Samuel 16:7 reminds us that God doesn't see things as we do. He doesn't
judge outward appearances, but He looks at the heart. How you view yourself
determines how far you will go in life. God made you the head and not the
tail; above only, and not beneath (Deuteronomy 28:13). You are fearfully and
wonderfully made (Psalm 139:14). You are more than enough. You are beauti-
ful, smart, strong and -- most of all -- His! Don't allow the world to ever make
you feel less than His definition of you. You are a daughter of the King! You
are loved and adored by Him.

Arise, walk boldly into your destiny and believe what Romans 8:30-31 states.
Through your acceptance of Jesus Christ as your Lord and Savior, God de-
clared you "not guilty," filled you with His goodness, gave you right standing
with Himself and promised you His Glory. He is so evidently for you that
nothing or no one can successfully be against you. There are plenty of oppos-
ing forces against you, as a Believer, but nothing can successfully overcome
you. Be encouraged. You have the greatest leader on your side and through
His strength and love, you can walk boldly against all the enemy's attacks and
know that you will not be defeated.

PRAYER

God, help me to see myself as you see me. Show me your plan and purpose for
my life. Lead me. I will obey and glorify You. In Jesus' name, Amen.

REFLECTION

Do you see yourself as God sees you? If not, what are some negative self-thought patterns that God is asking you to release? What is one thing you want to do/start this week to honor God and His purpose for your life?

_____

_____

_____

_____

_____

_____

_____

_____

_____

_____

_____

_____

_____

_____

_____

_____

_____

_____

_____

_____

_____

_____

His loves never fails.

Day 4

PURE UNDERSTANDING OF GOD'S LOVE

Read: Jeremiah 31: 1 – 3

"Long ago the Lord said to Israel: "I have loved you, my people, with an everlasting love. With unfailing love I have drawn you to myself."" - Jeremiah 31:3 NLT

I n this day and age, social media plays a huge role in our view of success. The non-stop social media posts – you know the ones featuring lavish romantic relationships, international vacations and attractive career trappings – can tempt us to become frustrated, worried or angry as we compare our lives to others. I can relate to this firsthand. Nonetheless, it's important to know that while you don't feel successful in an area of your life, God's great plan for your life doesn't depend on the world's definition of success. Jeremiah 29:11 states, "For I know the plans I have for you, says the Lord. They are plans for good and not for disaster, to give you a future and a hope." His plans for you are specific and unique to you. His plans are designed to prosper you far beyond just blessing you with your dream job, house, car or spouse. He wants you to prosper in all things, and be healthy, just as you are spiritually (3 John 1:2).

As a child, I learned that I had to be patient when waiting for my mother's freshly baked cupcakes to cool. If I grew impatient and tried to eat a cupcake while it was hot, I could get hurt. My mother's warnings to wait protected me from getting burned. In the same way, God protects you from receiving the things that you desire but are not good for you. He truly has your best interest at heart. When you trust and obey Him, you receive what you need and in-finitely more than you might ask or think (Ephesians 3:20).

I pray that when faced with opportunities to feel depressed or upset because you haven't achieved your idea of success, you instead choose to be joyful as you reflect on God's love for you. Not achieving those things does not mean you are not successful or loved. The greatest love of all is the everlasting love you receive from God every day. His love is enough to sustain you, no matter what you face. Allow Him to drive out your fears and bring you peace.

PRAYER

Father, reveal Your perfect, everlasting love to me. Draw me close, drive out my fear and make our relationship deep, strong and unshakable. Amen.

REFLECTION

Do you believe that God has your best interest at heart? What are you willing to surrender to God regarding your idea of success? Is your dream to get married by a certain age, have kids by a certain age and/or achieve C-suite career status by a certain time? How can you take steps to trust God and remain content in this season of your life?

_____

_____

_____

_____

_____

_____

_____

_____

_____

_____

_____

_____

_____

_____

_____

_____

_____

_____

_____

_____

_____

ENCOURAGEMENT
FOR THE JOURNEY

There is peace in the presence of God.

Day 5

PURE UNDERSTANDING OF GOD'S PEACE

Read: Mark 4:35 – 41

"He got up, rebuked the wind and said to the waves, "Quiet! Be still!" Then the wind died down and it was completely calm." - Mark 4:39 NLT

Mark 4:39 is the perfect reminder of what will happen when we invite God into the storms of our lives. He is so mighty that even the winds and waves obey Him. He calmed the fears of the disciples and allowed them to experience His peace. He wants to do the same for us.

I know there are times that you feel as though there is no hope or solution available for the storms you face. During these moments, it is imperative to place your faith in God and believe He is with you and that you will experience His peace. Now the peace I speak of brings inner stability, security and comfort like none other. It is possible for you to have it, and it is available to you! God promises to never leave or forsake you, and His constant presence is how you can experience His peace.

I'm not saying you will be exempt from having trouble in life, but you can rest assured knowing that God promised to be an ever-present help in times of trouble. Through His presence, you can experience His peace. Take heart and know that regardless of what storms may come, the One who has overcome the world dwells in you and defends you (John 16:33).

PRAYER

Thank You Jesus for Your constant presence and the peace You bring me. Amen.

REFLECTION

How do you react when you face trouble? Do you panic? Do you give way to discouragement? Do you give up? What change(s) can you make, starting today, to begin to experience God's peace in times of trouble?

_____

_____

_____

_____

_____

_____

_____

_____

_____

_____

_____

_____

_____

_____

_____

_____

_____

_____

_____

_____

_____

Erica N. Williams

God is your shield and protection.

Day 6

Pure Understanding of God's Protection

Read: Psalm 84

"For the Lord God is our sun and our shield. He gives us grace and glory. The Lord will withhold no good thing from those who do what is right. O Lord of Heaven's Armies, what joy for those who trust in you." - Psalm 84:11 NLT

When I first started my relationship with Christ, I often felt unworthy and worried that I had missed my blessings. These feelings always surfaced when I had to wait for God to fulfill His promises in my life. However, after digging into Scripture concerning this, I learned that my perception was a bit flawed.

God sometimes makes us wait so that He can develop sweet qualities within us. As a result, we can fully enjoy His blessings when it's time for us to receive them. If you receive them before you're ready, you won't be able to handle them.

Be encouraged during your seasons of waiting; know that God is being a good Father. He is omniscient and works in ways we don't understand. God is the Alpha and Omega who sees the end from the beginning (Isaiah 46:9-11). You must understand that your waiting is part of a bigger plan. He desires to protect you from that which means you no good. He also becomes your Glory by conforming you to His character, teaching you His wisdom and preparing for His power to shine through you so that others may be encouraged by your faith. So, whenever you feel unworthy or defeated, remember Psalm 84:11. God is your protector!

Prayer

Thank You, Father, for your protection. Bring to my remembrance the times you protected me from things that weren't good for me. Increase my faith so that I can believe You are behind the scenes working on my behalf. Amen.

REFLECTION

Do you know God as your protector? What personal memory do you have of His protection in your life? How does this memory affect your thoughts as you wait for Him to fulfill His promises to you?

_____

_____

_____

_____

_____

_____

_____

_____

_____

_____

_____

_____

_____

_____

_____

_____

_____

_____

_____

_____

God will
do infinitely
more than
you could
ever hope for
or imagine.
Don't give up!

Day 7

PURE UNDERSTANDING OF GOD'S POWER

Read: Ephesians 3:19 – 21

"Now all glory to God, who is able, through His mighty power at work within us, to accomplish infinitely more than we might ask or think." - Ephesians 3:20 NLT

At the beginning of each year, I dedicate time to fast, pray and seek God regarding the areas that should get my time and attention. As a result, I create a list of goals to accomplish during the year. While I achieve some goals early, by mid-year, there are still some I have yet to start. Some have been added, removed or added to the following year's to-do list. However, every time I achieve a goal, I'm able to look back and see how God used every experience to set the stage for His answers to my prayers. These moments help me trust God's timing and believe that no matter how big my dreams are, His dreams for me will always be bigger.

You may have dreams that appear far away because of the opposition on your journey. I want to encourage you today; regardless of what you face in life, don't give up on your dreams. I don't care how many no's you receive, who walks away or how tough things get. Don't give up!

God is faithful to fulfill His promises, but you must do your part. Seek Him. Live to honor Him. Serve others. Don't fall into the trap of comparison. Remain focused. Set a plan of action. If you fail, go back to the drawing board. Be patient. Be consistent. Be obedient. When God tells you to leave something or someone alone, do it without hesitation. Surround yourself with friends who are reliable and committed to seeing you win. Accountability is everything!

Never lose sight of God and His promises for your life. He can do infinitely more than you could ever ask or think. I'm a living witness. From the same supply that the Lord has blessed me, He will also bless, favor and provide for you (2 Corinthians 9:8).

PRAYER

Father, help me to hold fast to Your promises. Fill me with faith and help me experience Your power in my life in unprecedented ways. Amen.

REFLECTION

Do you understand that the same power that raised Jesus from the dead lives in you (Philippians 3:10-11)? Are you avoiding something or someone that God is asking you to revisit? What or who is it?

_____

_____

_____

_____

_____

_____

_____

_____

_____

_____

_____

_____

_____

_____

_____

_____

_____

_____

_____

_____

_____

_____

"Study this Book of Instruction continually. Meditate on it day and night so you will be sure to obey everything in it. Only then will you prosper and succeed in all you do."

KEY VERSES

As you become familiar with God's Word and learn His promises, you can begin to draw strength from them during times of discouragement. I've provided a few verses to start. Personalize these key verses in the spaces provided below and try to memorize them so you can quickly recall them when needed.

Psalm 27:14

_____

_____

_____

_____

Philippians 4:13-14

_____

_____

_____

_____

Jude 1:24-25

_____

_____

_____

_____

Philippians 4:8

_____

_____

_____

_____

Matthew 19:26

_____

_____

_____

_____

"Don't worry about anything; instead, pray about everything. Tell God what you need and thank Him for all He has done."

FOCUS PRAYER

No matter what things look like or how tough your circumstances seem, speak things that are not as though they are in Jesus' name. Seek God for guidance on your journey. He will help you remain focused on Him and fulfill the destiny He has created just for you.

Below is a prayer that you can start off praying in the morning. It's good to declare positive words over yourself throughout the day and before you go to bed at night. Work on declaring who you are and the promises of God aloud and in prayer.

Father God, in the name of Jesus, I pray that all hindering spirits of distraction, ungodly attraction, confusion, delusion, and double-mindedness are removed from my life. I have the mind of Christ. I am steadfast in the things of the Lord and focused on the mark that He has for me in life. I am stable and steadfast in my calling and will not miss the high calling on my life because of attacks on my mind. I will advance and prosper in every position or project I under-take. Nothing will hinder, prevent or delay God's will for my life. Fear is far from me, because God has not given me a spirit of fear, but of power, love and self-discipline. I am strong, bold, and courageous in Christ. I am convinced that no weapon turned against me will succeed, because God is for me—who can be against me? The favor of the Lord is upon me. God will guide my steps and lead me in all my affairs. All that I set my hands to do will prosper and succeed. I am healed from all emotional, physical, mental, and spiritual sicknesses and diseases. I decree that I am saved, sanctified, and satisfied in Jesus' name, Amen.

Prayer Requests and Answers

One effective tool I use to help me in times of discouragement is my prayer journal. My faith and trust in God are always reinforced when I look at my past prayer requests and how God has answered them.

Use the following pages to record your personal prayer requests to God. You may also note the ways in which God answers. You can refer to them as proof of what God has done in your life, to remind you to thank Him when He answers your prayers, and to strengthen your faith to trust God and His timing in the days ahead.

Prayer Request

Date: _____

_____

_____

_____

_____

_____

_____

Answer

Date: _____

_____

_____

_____

_____

_____

_____

Prayer Request

Date: _____

_____

_____

_____

_____

_____

_____

_____

_____

Answer

Date: _____

_____

_____

_____

_____

_____

_____

_____

_____

_____

Prayer Request

Date: _____

_____

_____

_____

_____

_____

_____

_____

_____

Answer

Date: _____

_____

_____

_____

_____

_____

_____

_____

_____

Prayer Request

Date: _____

_____

_____

_____

_____

_____

_____

_____

_____

Answer

Date: _____

_____

_____

_____

_____

_____

_____

_____

_____

Prayer Request

Date: _____

_____

_____

_____

_____

_____

_____

_____

_____

Answer

Date: _____

_____

_____

_____

_____

_____

_____

_____

_____

Prayer Request

Date: _____

_____

_____

_____

_____

_____

_____

_____

_____

Answer

Date: _____

_____

_____

_____

_____

_____

_____

_____

_____

Prayer Request

Date: _____

_____

_____

_____

_____

_____

_____

_____

_____

Answer

Date: _____

_____

_____

_____

_____

_____

_____

_____

_____

Quick Reference

Accepting Others	Acts 10:34-35
Anxiety	Philippians 4:6-7; 1 Peter 5:7
Beauty	1 Peter 3:3-5; Ecclesiastes 3:11
Children	Ephesians 6:1; Colossians 3:20; Psalm 45:2
Conflict	Proverbs 15:1; 1 Peter 3:8-9
Contentment	Philippians 4:11-13
Creativity	Romans 12:6-8
Depression	Psalm 55:22; John 14:1
Disappointment	Luke 6:21
Discipleship	Galatians 2:20
Encouragement	Joshua 1:6-8
Eternal Life	John 10:27-28
Faith	Hebrews 11:1; Matthew 17:20
Finances	Hebrews 13:5; Psalm 23:1
Forgiveness	2 Chronicles 7:14; Mark 11:25; Colossians 3:13
Friendship	Proverbs 17:17; Ecclesiastes 4:9-10
Frustration	Romans 8:31-32; Psalm 34:19
God's Presence	Matthew 28:20; Isaiah 41:10
Grace	2 Chronicles 30:9; Hebrews 4:15-16
Grief and Death	Psalm 23:4; Matthew 5:4
Guidance	Psalm 32:8; Proverbs 3:5-6
Holiness	1 Thessalonians 4:7; 2 Peter 1:3; Philippians 4:8
Honesty	Psalm 145:18; Proverbs 16:13; Luke 16:10
Hope	Isaiah 40:31; Ephesians 3:20-21; Jeremiah 29

Hospitality	Romans 12:13; Matthew 25:35-40; 1 Peter 4:9
Joy	Nehemiah 8:10; Philippians 4:4
Kindness	Ephesians 4:32; Proverbs 11:16
Love	John 3:16; Romans 8:39
Loving Others	1 Corinthians 13:4-6; Leviticus 19:18
Mercy	Deuteronomy 4:31; Luke 6:36
Peace	Proverbs 16:7; John 14:27; Psalm 4:8
Perspective	1 Samuel 16:7
Praise	Psalm 149
Prayer	Matthew 6:9-13
Relationships	Ephesians 4:2-3
Restoration	John 21:15-19
Rest	Exodus 33:14
Self-Worth	Jeremiah 1:5; 1 Corinthians 6:19-20; Matthew 10:29-31
Speech	Ephesians 4:29
Talents & Abilities	Deuteronomy 8:18; 1 Peter 4:10
Thankfulness	Psalm 7:17; Psalm 34:1
Trust	Nahum 1:7; Romans 10:11
Values	Galatians 5:22-23
Wisdom	Colossians 1:9-11
Work	Colossians 3:23

About Erica

After losing her father at the age of 11, Erica N. Williams experienced grief and spent years trying to fill this void by looking for love in all the wrong places. She hoped that she could find a man who would love her unconditionally and not leave her.

One day, Erica clearly heard the Lord speak to her. God told her that He loved her, and He had great plans for her life. God wanted to use Erica in a mighty way for His glory but only if she made herself available to Him. On that day, Erica said, "yes," to God and His plans for her life. And she has never been the same.

On September 12, 2011, Erica made a vow of celibacy and two weeks later was baptized. She refused to let the death of her father or the difficulties of her life define her. Instead, she clung to God's Word and His vision for her. Since that time, she has endeavored to share the gospel of Jesus Christ with whomever would listen. Erica has also encouraged others to focus on God and fulfill His desires for their lives.

A graduate of the University of South Carolina Upstate, Erica earned a Master of Public Administration (MPA) degree from Georgia Southern University. She is a member of Harvest Life Church in Woodbridge, Virginia where she serves in Leadership and the Music and Fine Arts Ministry.

Connect with Erica daily, follow her ministry schedule and receive Biblical encouragement:

Website: www.ericanwilliams.com
Facebook: fb.me/officialericanwilliams
Instagram: @EricaNWilliams
Twitter: @EricaNWilliams

About Journey To Purity

Erica N. Williams is the founder of Journey to Purity, based in Woodbridge, Virginia.

If you were encouraged by *Don't Give Up* and desire to grow spiritually with the support of a community of like-minded women, we can help.

Journey to Purity provides ready-to-use curricula and trainings designed to help women of all ages overcome spiritual, physical, mental and emotional struggles. With the aid of these resources, they can build a network of encouragement, accountability and support among other women with the same goal of fulfilling God's desire for their lives.

To find out how you can join a local Journey to Purity group or start one in your area, visit www.journeytopuritymovement.com.

To inquire about having Erica speak at your event, visit www.ericanwilliams.com and click on "Contact."

www.ingramcontent.com/pod-product-compliance
Lightning Source LLC
Chambersburg PA
CBHW072055040426
42447CB00012BB/3131